Ghosts Hold U1 Rainfa

Rhianna Levi

Ghosts Hold Umbrellas In Rainfall

Rhianna Levi
Edited by Black Pear Press

Published in 2023 by Black Pear Press
www.blackpear.net
Copyright © Rhianna Levi

ISBN 978-1-916910-00-3

Cover image by Tony Judge & DALL·E 2
and Design by Black Pear Press

Black Pear Press

Dedication

This collection is dedicated to all those who acknowledge the thinness of the spectral veil—the fusing variations of life and death.

Introduction

My fascination with the spirits that live among us has come to be through the personal experiences that I and others have had. Growing up, I have learnt how to be comfortable with the unknown and unexplainable, giving myself permission to be curious about the multi spectral complexity of life and death.

Everyday, we are visited by ghosts, whether that be through memories or through ghostly encounters. Each day, we make a conscious decision to either ignore our spiritual neighbours or greet them with a nod or conversation.

I wished to explore this further and as a result, here it is in the form of my Worcestershire Poet Laureate collection. The work in this poetry collection is inspired by different types of hauntings across the world. Some of these hauntings will be recognisable from the offset, others more subjective.

Either way, this collection hopes to give readers a new perspective; spirits have always lived among us and will continue to do so. Like us, they have stories, emotions and movement. Doors between what we perceive to be life and death are actually very alike, and we should honour it.

Remain your authentic spooky self.

Rhianna x

Facebook: Rhianna Levi
Twitter: @RhiannaLevi98
Instagram: @RhiannaLevi98

'We should all treasure everything because spirits might exist there, and we should treasure everything because there is a kind of life to everything.'
~ Hayao Miyazaki

Contents

Dedication...iii

Introduction...iv

Contents..vi

City of Crusty Bone...1

Blip..2

St Mary's Church..3

Placemat Greed on Marbled Floor...............................4

No Answer...5

Sit in Lone Chapels more Often...................................6

Bodmin Never Rests...7

Freelan Oscar Stanley's Jazz Service 8

Commandery Schedule 9

Masking Criminality...10

Eyam's Memorial 11

Powick Flares in War 12

This Home is not Mine...13

Beauty in Past's Presence...14

By All in Salem..15

Her Lighthouse Haunting...16

Surrounding You 17

The Damned Dam..18

Elemental Leap 19

Waverley Fixation Maze..20

Signing in..21

A Resting Place is not Always where We Fall Asleep 22

Holiness...23

Cross My Lungs 24

His Name is Kieran...25

Semi-colon Rocking Chair...26

Heist...27

What Others Say 28

Publications...29

City of Crusty Bone

A city of bones, these ruins engineered;
12 years of directed cart after cart.
Not so swiftly integrated,
sharp calcium made these walls.
Secrets refrained from being hindered—
inspired to nourish.

So, below precious Paris passion,
not above graveyard lanterns,
there is only so far that people are allowed to go
in curiosity of this harkening city of bones.

If people do not wish to lose a tightened grip of their sense,
they must remember the path to tread
solitude is not bliss at an alleyway that ignorant people solicit.

With a hiss, anyone can become melded to a crucifix city of
   crusty bone.
Catacomb homes, stripped of easy sleep.

Blip

Tongues rusting.
Spectators multiply in these earthy conditions
foolishly dancing in hopes of catching a dream or two—
do they sleep, or are they stationed to curve their antennas
away from the burial mound?
Rustles wish to click the abandoned lighter
when they acquire a hazy,
placid sleeping nest.

St Mary's Church

A survivor from the fires of the underworld as a fluid muse
it stands tall even in its crumbling décor,
establishes a tranquil peacefulness for all those weary visitors
protected by familiar enchantments of all those loved and lost.

Stories are sweet nothings in stone walls,
swallowed by mother nature, appearing in melodies
entrusted with beauty, dedication, comfort.

Who knew a derelict church in Tintern would purify hearts,
lifetimes deep?
My father spoke of chronicles as we went on across the
    uneven stone ground;
I am inclined to agree with his position,
visiting a cemetery is an enriching activity.

Placemat Greed on Marbled Floor

Thoughts muddle across marble floor,
the breathing profile seeks blood bags that are full,
a more metallic taste than absorbing golden coils.

But that is not enough for the presence at the door,
more adventures might be performed.
And with that,
room to dusty room,
the effigy lust for oddities—amazements not effortlessly
    clocked.
Not enough to have been seen by.

And as day met its end
all that was left in a side room with a vengeful chest
were two glazed eyes of gold that had met its wishful end.

Periodically, far too much has been seen.

No Answer

Simplicity never has been gauged here
while, unwilling, blood runs
out of the room.
If you are on your way to a musty grave,
secure sleep elsewhere,
but not here,
in halls of suspicious and brooding rust of instruments
failing to deliver life.

Blood clots will manifest in a phantasmagoric haze
comforting you to the elasticated end,
and if dare
you will wake up here
in the Infirmary's committee of the somewhat dead.

You may not receive an answer from that ringing telephone
    in your struggling ear,
or a soaked bandage for a wretched heartbreak
revisiting your bubonic fear at a fruitless daybreak
that fades across the same drifting ward ceiling descried with a
drawn bow.

You meet swallowing eyes for the terminating sigh
that swiftly takes you backwards
into the talkative nocturnal.

Sit in Lone Chapels more Often

Chapel praying hands in objection of freezing feet,
find kindness in yourself to set your medical turmoil free.

Sorrow and gratitude drawn together with meditation,
we are not the same beings that drift in an Infirmary's
murmuring chapel.

Bodmin Never Rests

There is a commodity,
ruthlessly intrusive,
hunting in dimness, dankness, darkness
creeping steadily on the fresh backs of those rightfully wary.

Fear makes the most lustrous of feasts,
an appropriate pairing with impressions of a snapping noose
in winter's sneeze.
Do you not notice the biting on your already bruising heels?

Store caution on the weight that is now perusing
your shoulder blades.
Bodmin stalks you to bed,
unwilling to rest.
We've learnt the skill of whistling at the turning of a strange
    end.

Freelan Oscar Stanley's Jazz Service

I'll pirouette in circles of jazz music in hue notes,
I care less that I do not know how.
Lips nourished in cooling wine of mountain frostbite
and indigo lies converse in delight
with hotel neighbours during another stay.

No knowledge of what my directed death day will be,
those surrounding me do not remember theirs,
and yet
they have decided to stay and play in all seasons of founded
    Colorado.

Humour moulded at the expense of guests,
meets with opportune jest.
I entreat those in high heaven above
to make this my rapture—
cascaded to honourable hotel service.

Commandery Schedule

There's never time in civil war,
no contract signed in order to live more.
The Commandery clock hits the talking walls,
spitting glass across the Great Hall.

There are those here who saw it from across built beams,
blood stains splatted their Christian names.
Free time given, all at once,
at the cost of rarely, if ever, being seen.

Resentment comes with time's inequitable treatment,
but there is desire to play in a museum re-enactment.

Their cheerful chuckles echo ear to ear,
busy spooks move items in rooms far and near.

Masking Criminality

Metallic masks of potted shame for crimes committed in jest.
A community who viewed them as wraiths of murder, theft,
corruptive horror of human thought.
Life is not bought, but death in the masks is paid in fortune,
reserved for medical history.

The boat takes the masked soul across the wall,
the unknown person remains obscure,
their identity stripped away in a realm against meetings
of forgiveness across crooked medical tables.

Fables remain of these anonymous masks,
no names received.
We can guess who they were and know their brains
may have formed differently;
brittle masks of the undead in museums they remain.
Bare faces materialise at the place they felt the crunching
noose and the Reaper's trusted hooves.

Eyam's Memorial

Plagued village of death;
bones of suffered dirt.
Compassion saved Queen's England
at the hands of a village's declared death pact.

Human acts made in fear, behind all we hold dear.
400 hitched their souls to the highway door,
in hopes for others to be awoken reborn.

Eyam was consumed by the pestilence;
corrupted by the devil's disease.
Swollen lungs, bubonic war, a rat-infested lure.
They toiled for others to bear witness at dawn.

These black spots of mortality mounted,
fevered with each strain of pain.
People experienced no gain for themselves,
apart from faith in better days

and a tranquil death that could save others in the thousands.

Remember their selfless gaze,
as they were absorbed by the spectacle
of Death's ongoing maze.

Powick Flares in War

Powick became the unvalued edifice,
hoping lullabies of compassion would soothe torments.
Human minds that became too much for public display,
made their way via train to Powick's flowered lawn,
often where they remained.

It paid no heed how much people prayed
to no longer be a follower of fear,
humming sweet thoughts to oneself
ignoring visuals of congested hospital corridors.
It was too real,
pained further by trauma's fluorescent steel.

Too many people of Powick Hospital
have undeniably been forgotten,
identities smouldered within stone walls.
Would that stone talked beyond four walls.

This Home is not Mine

Tainted nails in grooming roots
disease in succeeding voices.
I sit in departing grass crafted around an apparent home.

It is no longer my own home.

Owners are the maggots—infested with the house's bones.
Roommates with a vengeance and shadow—I am yet to obtain
the figure's name.

This place has more than rewinding halls.
Corrupted twisting puzzles are a game that it adores to play.
Nowadays I sleep in all black.
I ignore the many eyes behind.

Nihilism used to be friend, but now I am bound—
iron chains that are no longer seen;
a giggle that pulls my silky spine.
This relapse from guilt has caused my eyes to wilt.

Beauty in Past's Presence

We walk the way to become ghosts of present's extraordinary
    foregone.
We remain, barely seen, yet still here,
longing not to flee, but to persist in encounters
of appreciated present feeling.

Spirits see wonders in medical advances,
shedding water droplets down towards cheeks and chin;
indebted for lives saved, progressed, regained.
Unearthed education shimmering across the infirmary halls,
the wider wonders of a marigold city.

In scenarios where the sky has propelled ragged forces of
    human nature,
spirits that dabbled in medical fields always remain.
A fortunate happening with no association to deeds
of committed dimming.

What an amazement medical souls have always been.

By All in Salem

A figure is liquidised in shadows;
it lapses to its own momentum,
seeks answers from all in Salem;
those shadows are growing, time is slowing.

No mourning, but indignation
towards all of those in Salem.
They dreamed of keeping their breath.

To not be swallowed by discrimination and hallucinations
by those who suffer such delusions.

Pitchforks are poison
and black emptiness is in those eyes.
Tears are not welcome
by those in Salem.

Her Lighthouse Haunting

We have all seen the lighthouse,
sought the colours within,
companioned with solitude sweeping ocean's deep.

She is huddled in the interiors,
that lighthouse is her own.
Years, and years, and years.

And there she prevails through the windows,
as boats seek the bounded passage.
Dictating each being's fate:
Scarlet skin, daggered nails,
delight in every ferocious water drip.

Surrounding You

It's not just me in this maze
levitating with an unfound purpose,
grazing the floor with my superior dress,
clearing up history's mess.
Something else lures here,
lusts for open skin to crawl in fright.
A lover of possession, but not of
a Christian name.

                                     Targeting

backs that play victim to forceful trickery

trespassing on its rotting and vanishing grave.
A tower destabilised does not wish to enrich
rhymes of romantic spiritual connections,
instead, it urges you to arrive at a picnic,
but all that is served is a decaying rattle snake.

                                        Not

every entity is warm blooded.

The Damned Dam[1] Donation

Manpower brought forward the scuffled dam;
dollar bills fired forward the resistance to fear,
but whistling calls upon the counting bodies
flayed in flashing floods of the dead—
yielded towards
and against bolted stone.

Falling to an unseen obscurity,
manners of farewell rise,
as safety precautions nose dive.
A life cycle of the blind
leading the plucky mind.

In America's digression of sensibility
a heated coal depression;
who can say what gathered the dead?
A lusting against economical stability,
the dam reaps a hideous, luring centre

---

[1] *https://ghostcitytours.com/las-vegas/haunted-vegas/hoover-dam/*

Elemental Leap

Hefty knocks to the chest,
tooth bites mark the unsuspecting thigh.
A troublesome handling of the psyche,
sharpened until everyone breaks down and cries.

Supremacy is no result of copper coinage,
instead it closes an opening to heaven's door.

Did this elemental arrive to set eroding chaos to the walls?
Did it retreat to the halls,
sucking on tears of bloodshed
that rotted into a physical hoard?

Ruthless deeds reign the dead,
an urge for bestowed dread;
wickedness is a shady spheroid
and it dreams of coming
for your feathered dreams and appearance.

Waverley Fixation Maze

Push that chair this way,
not over there.
Think our way,
not individually.

No, you are not freed from this contract
when you suffer to your death.
You were considered lowly in life
and even now that is so.

You wish to escape?
Be at peace with your name and solitary brain?
Be away from this crusty place?
That will not do.

Get used to crawling underneath
this hospital's spiritually occupied hooves.
Aim lower to the tiles,
place yourself in the position of Grimm's new pet
hate.

Signing in

They have no intentions of departing,
they memorise their past times of hopscotch,
take advantage of moving things unseen,
ruffle people's hair with familiar ease.

They've stared at the bizarre actions of the living,
have not had enough exposure to socialising with ghosts
who prod in amusement,
the opposite of wishing to express harm.

Please steer clear from the resident incubus,
it is less sociable and appreciative of our guests.
If you have any queries,
please do not hesitate to contact the front desk,
or call out to your allocated ghostly roommate.

A Resting Place is not Always where We Fall Asleep

We make the kind request, remember us for who we were
and push away images of the forest plain.
We left our throbbing heart and rocketing thoughts there,
but we are bonded to you for ages yet to come.

We could apologise that we left,
but for us, it was the correct next step.
Forgive us for the abrupt nature of our exit,
but invisible tears fell beyond the upholding presence
   of our neck.
We promise to visit,
to assist you in your errands and recollections of loving days.

Live on for yourselves and us,
lock the memory of that forest away,
we found eternal sleep in its growth as we lived,
but we've returned to your side,
the dark days have diffused.

Holiness

He acted on their prayers once.
Their hope, his reinforced energy bellowing through hollow
holes that sat upon their heads.

Not enough to let them go though.
He once heard their calls, but in developing opaqueness
their God has stepped away: thorns in arms.

A hunt of a more living type of faithfulness,
aghast to blinking sanatorium statues.

Cross My Lungs

Passerby
valves meet
dehydrated
deceased
Dorothy.

She lets slip a meek wail to find the faceless bundle of joy that
gathered in her enlarged rose womb. Virtue did not protect
the babe or the young respiring fern

from a
wheezing
world; their
lungs carved
to the cross.

His Name is Kieran

Death is a thorn in the sides of many,
trespassing on those held dearly.

When he left, unicorns across galaxies fell silent.

It was the first time these beings experienced mourning.
Cotton candy smile, artistry demonstrated through mastery.

The finest unicorn that one was privileged to meet.

Time could be considered a villain, but appreciation for him
made our ambitions dive into ocean space,
not anchored with acrylic fear.

He skips humorously with us still in the biscuit tin,
Hawaiian shirts in abundance.

Semi-colon Rocking Chair

I'm no saviour of daisies.
I'm just waiting for these holes to tie together in a pretty bow,
my perfume releasing itself randomly in the ecosphere.

Fortune comes in picking when people notice me and where;
I steal time with feet up on a pitching chair
where the sunbeams screech through me at a disruptive speed.

And I do not mind being a ghost to most
because I'm able to deliver an infinite possibility
that death is no empty car seat.
It can be a regal new verdict, not a dead-end appointment.

Heist

He burns his pulse in two so he can hold her cooling hand
with the nerve endings he bunched into a withering bouquet.
He views "Till death do us part" as a schoolboy challenge he
   created
in silent haste.
You'd think he would excel in the exercise of parting ways,
but his heart has never felt blue before.
She's his favourite ghost heist,
night after night—
in the rupturing skies and the woodland.

What Others Say

'Rhianna Levi's latest collection promises us an insight into the "multi-spectral complexity of life and death", a promise kept with startling brilliance by the youngest ever Worcestershire Poet Laureate. Her poems take us on journeys from Paris catacombs to desolate West Country moorlands, places close to home. Levi pays tribute to a much-loved local poet and friend with a loving and empathetic touch.

There is a very real sense of corporeal veils fluttering and following the shades of shadowed life as we read, showing the music that exists in both life and death, accompanied by playful spooks and saddened souls.'

Leena Batchelor *Worcestershire Poet Laureate 2020-2021*

'In our ancient realm, we are surrounded by hints and resonances of the past—things intuited or half-seen; the quiet sad horrors of an old infirmary or an empty chapel, or the lingering sense of tragic history that still persists for those who can hear the whispers. This is a memorable and truly haunting collection.'

Suz Winspear *Worcestershire Poet Laureate 2016-2017*

28

Publications

Mortal Veins (Independently published, 2023)
Life's Wonders (Black Pear Press, 2023)
Growing Bones and Freckles (Independently published, 2023)